HOW'S THE WEATHER?

It's Raining!

Julie Richards

Smart Apple Media

Smart Apple Media
1980 Lookout Drive
North Mankato
Minnesota 56003

Library of Congress Cataloging-in-Publication Data

Richards, Julie.
 It's raining! / by Julie Richards.
 p. cm. — (How's the weather?)
 Includes bibliographical references and index.
 ISBN 1-58340-536-4 (alk. paper)
 1. Rain and rainfall—Juvenile literature. [1. Rain and rainfall. 2. Weather.] I. Title.
 QC924.7.R53 2004
 551.57'7—dc22   2003070415

First Edition
9 8 7 6 5 4 3 2 1

First published in 2004 by
MACMILLAN EDUCATION AUSTRALIA PTY LTD
627 Chapel Street, South Yarra 3141

Associated companies and representatives throughout the world.

Copyright © Julie Richards 2004

Edited by Vanessa Lanaway
Page layout by Domenic Lauricella
Illustrations by Melissa Webb
Photo research by Legend Images

Printed in China

Acknowledgements

The author and the publisher are grateful to the following for permission to reproduce copyright material:

Cover photograph: children in rain, courtesy of Getty Images/Stone.

Wayne Lawler/Auscape, pp. 15, 17; Australian Picture Library/Corbis, p. 8; Digital Vision, pp. 9, 20, 21; Getty Images/Image Bank, pp. 10, 14; Getty Images/Stone, pp. 1, 4, 16; Photodisc, pp. 5, 7, 18, 22, 26, 27, 29; Photolibrary.com/Index Stock, pp. 11, 19; Photolibrary.com/SPL, pp. 6, 23; Terry Oakley/The Picture Source, p. 30; © Sergio Piumatti, p. 25; Reuters, p. 28.

While every care has been taken to trace and acknowledge copyright, the publisher tenders their apologies for any accidental infringement where copyright has proved untraceable. Where the attempt has been unsuccessful, the publisher welcomes information that would redress the situation.

Please note

At the time of printing, the Internet addresses appearing in this book were correct. Owing to the dynamic nature of the Internet, however, we cannot guarantee that all these addresses will remain correct.

Contents

How's the Weather?

Have you noticed how the weather always changes? You might feel warm sunshine or a cool breeze, or see rain or hear thunder. Weather changes from day to day and **season** to season.

These children are having fun on a rainy day.

4

The Amazon Jungle is very green because it gets a lot of rain.

The weather varies from place to place, too. In some places, it rains every day. Other places, such as deserts, have hardly any rain. Most places have both rainy and dry weather. How's the weather where you live?

Rain

Rain is drops of water that fall from the sky. Drizzling rain has tiny drops that fall slowly. Bigger, heavy raindrops fall fast. Rain that stops and starts is called a shower.

Large raindrops hit the ground with a big splat.

Different shaped raindrops on a leaf.

A raindrop is not a teardrop shape as many people think. Raindrops are round, and as they fall they are flattened and stretched into other shapes.

A Rainy Day

On a rainy day the sky fills with grey clouds, and then it rains, making everything wet. The rain fills holes to make puddles and can turn soil muddy. The air smells fresh.

Heavy rain can make puddles and muddy ground.

rain

Rain falling from dark thunderstorm clouds.

Sometimes thunderstorms bring heavy rain.
You might also see lightning flash in the sky,
and then hear deep, rumbling thunder.

Rainy Day Gear

What do you wear on a rainy day? It can be fun to put on a raincoat, hat, and rubber boots. Then you can go outside and jump in puddles.

Rainy day gear helps keep you dry.

Do you put these things on when you go out on a rainy day?

And there's one piece of gear that you will always need when the rain comes down— an umbrella!

Where Does Rain Come From?

Rain is part of the **water cycle**. This cycle uses water again and again.

Rain falls when clouds get too heavy.

Sun

4 The water drops join together to form clouds.

3 As it rises, the water vapor cools and turns back into water drops.

1 Sunshine turns water into a gas called water vapor.

2 Water vapor rises into the air.

Rain soaks into the soil and trickles underground. Some rain flows into streams and street drains, where it is carried back to the rivers and oceans.

Clouds

5 When the cloud gets too heavy, rain falls.

6 Rivers flow back to the ocean and the cycle begins again.

Ocean

Rainy Seasons

Winter and spring are usually wetter than summer and fall. Spring rains help plants to grow into food for animals. In places where winter is very cold, rain falls as snow.

Spring rain helps the grass to grow for lambs to eat.

Heavy rain pours down nearly every day in the wet season.

Places that have only a wet and a dry season are hot all year. During the wet season, powerful winds called monsoons push gigantic rain clouds across the sky. Rain can pour down for days at a time.

15

Built for Rain

Houses often have sloped roofs for rain to run down into gutters and pipes. Gutters are also built in streets to carry water into drains. The drains then take the water out to rivers and oceans.

These roofs are sloped so that rain will run down into the gutters and pipes.

gutter

pipe

These houses are built on stilts to keep them above the water.

People living in places with high rainfall often build their houses on **stilts**. This stops water getting into their houses. They often use raised walkways or boats to get around.

17

We Need Rain

People, plants, and animals need water to survive. Rain brings fresh water for people and animals to drink. Plants use their roots to take up the rainwater from underground.

A group of zebras drinking at a waterhole.

The rain helps this crop stay healthy.

Nearly all our food comes from farms, rivers, and seas. Farmers depend on rain to grow **crops** and for their animals. Rain fills rivers and oceans, where fish live and breed.

Too Much Rain

As much rain falls, it can cause rivers and to overflow onto land. Floods can cause damage to bridges and buildings, and farmers can lose their crops.

Too much heavy rain has flooded these homes.

Not Enough Rain

If not enough rain falls, the soil becomes dry it turns to dust. Plants dry up and di and farm animals have little or nothing This is called a **drought**.

This earth is so dry it has cracked.

Dangerous Rain

Acid rain forms in clouds when dangerous chemicals are released into the air from cars, factories, and power stations. These chemicals mix with raindrops to make acid rain.

This power plant is releasing chemicals into the air.

The chemicals in acid rain eat into buildings and statues.

Acid rain can poison forests, rivers, and lakes, and kill fish and other animals. Many countries have passed laws to keep the air in cities cleaner to protect the environment.

Forecasting Rain

Scientists who **forecast** weather are called meteorologists. They use computers and look at **satellite** photos to find rain clouds. This information is used to forecast weather.

Symbols on weather maps show us what kind of weather is coming.

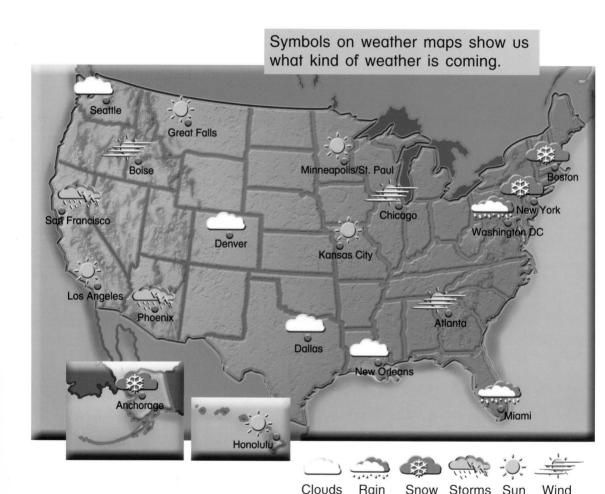

Clouds · Rain · Snow · Storms · Sun · Wind

The markings on this rain gauge show how much rain has fallen.

Meteorologists collect and measure rain in a **rain gauge**. Meteorologists also use **radar** to look inside clouds. Radar shows them how much rain might fall from the cloud.

Rainbows

On a rainy day, you might see a rainbow spread across the sky. When the sun shines through raindrops, the light breaks up into bands of different colors.

Sometimes you can only see part of a rainbow.

A rainbow has been made by the sun shining through this waterfall.

To see a rainbow, stand with your back to the sun and the rain falling in front of you. Then look at the sky and find the rainbow.

27

Rainy Sayings

People use weather sayings and words to describe everyday things.

I'll take a raincheck.

People say this when they want to do something later. The saying began when a baseball game was rained out and fans were given a raincheck ticket so they could attend another game.

It's raining cats and dogs.

People say this to describe very heavy rain. It's possible that ancient people believed that cats and dogs could make bad weather happen.

If the rain gets heavier, this baseball game may be rained out.

Weather Wonders

Did you know?

⭐ The wettest place on Earth is Mount Wai'ale'ale in Hawaii. It gets enough rain to cover six adults standing on each other's shoulders.

⭐ A dinosaur might have drunk our water. For billions of years, Earth has been using the same water. It is used again and again through the water cycle.

⭐ The driest place on Earth is the Atacama Desert in South America. The rainfall there in the last 50 years measures less than the length of your thumbnail.

Try This!

Ask a parent or teacher for help.

Make a mini water cycle

⭐ Fill two empty jars with water.

⭐ Cover one with a lid or plastic food wrap.

⭐ Leave both jars in a warm, sunny place for a day.

⭐ Look at the inside of the lid or food wrap.

The water droplets on the lid or food wrap are like the ones that make clouds. When the droplets are heavy, they will fall back into the jar, just like rain. The water in the uncovered jar has risen into the air.

Glossary

crops	plants grown for food
drought	when no rain falls for a long time
forecast	to know what kind of weather is coming
radar	a way of looking at faraway objects
rain gauge	an instrument used to measure how much rain has fallen
satellite	a small spacecraft that circles Earth and takes photographs
season	a part of the year that has its own kind of weather
stilts	long poles that are pushed deep into the ground
water cycle	the way water is used again and again

Index

Weather on the Web

Here are some Web sites that you might like to look at:
http://ga.water.usgs.gov/edu/watercycle2ndgrade.html
http://www.ucar.edu/educ_outreach/webweather/
http://www.wxdude.com

12/04